The ARTS

LITERATURE

Brian Williams

STECK-VAUGHN
LIBRARY
A Division of Steck-Vaughn Company
Austin, Texas

The Arts

Architecture
Dance
Design
Literature
The Movies
Music
Painting and Sculpture
Photography
Theater

Cover illustration: Dickens's Dream painted by R.W. Buss 1872–73.

Series and Book Editor: Rosemary Ashley
Designer: David Armitage
Consultant: Trevor Griffiths,
Department of Language and Literature,
Polytechnic of North London

**Published in the United States in 1991 by Steck Vaughn
Co., Austin, Texas,** a subsidiary of National Education
Corporation.

First published in 1989 by
Wayland (Publishers) Limited

Library of Congress Cataloging-in-Publication Data

Williams, Brian.
   Literature / Brian Williams.
      p.   cm. — (The Arts)
   Includes bibliographical references and index.
   Summary: Examines the history of literature from the oral
tradition of prehistoric people to modern times.
   ISBN 0-8114-2365-4
   1. Literature—History and criticism—Juvenile literature.
[1. Literature—History and criticism.]   I. Title   II. Series:
Arts (Austin, Tex.)
PN524.W57   1990
809—dc20   90-36113
                                                  CIP
                                                  AC

Typeset by Multifacit Graphics, Keyport, NJ
Printed in Italy
Bound in the United States by Lake Book, Melrose Park, IL
   1 2 3 4 5 6 7 8 9 0 CA 95 94 93 92 91

Contents

1 What is Literature?

"You can never be wise unless you love reading," said Dr. Samuel Johnson (1709–84), one of Britain's most famous literary figures. But how is literature different from other kinds of writing? Literature includes creative writing, such as stories, novels, poems, and plays, and many other forms of writing, such as biography (a person's life story), history, travel books, geography, natural history, science, and reference books of many types. Even advertising "sales literature" has an imaginative input, but a printed directory, the phone book for example, can only record. Literature does more; it attempts through language to describe and explore human experience.

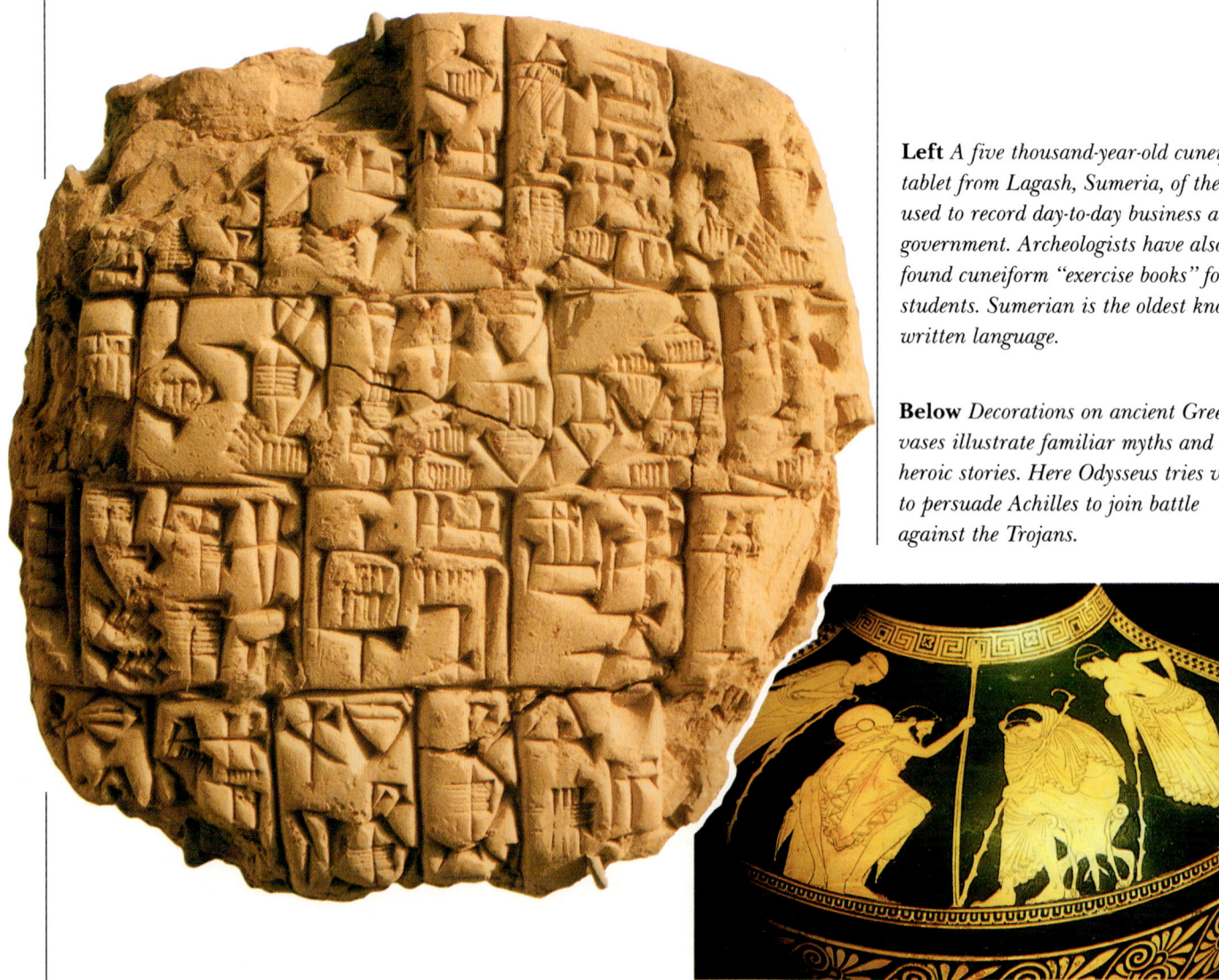

Left *A five thousand-year-old cuneiform tablet from Lagash, Sumeria, of the kind used to record day-to-day business and government. Archeologists have also found cuneiform "exercise books" for students. Sumerian is the oldest known written language.*

Below *Decorations on ancient Greek vases illustrate familiar myths and heroic stories. Here Odysseus tries vainly to persuade Achilles to join battle against the Trojans.*

Origins

Literature could not begin until there was language, the spoken form of communication unique to human beings. But although the word "literature" means "that which is written," literature encompasses more than written language. Cave dwellers thousands of years ago told stories, and these stories were handed down from parent to child. In this way oral (spoken) literature developed.

The oral tradition is still strong. Ask older people to reminisce about their youth—World War II (1939–45), perhaps—and their recall will often be lively and spontaneous, one memory stirring another. Ask another person to write down an account of the same events, and they may be unable to recount them in such an entertaining way. Often people find it easier to express themselves in speech than in writing. Many of the fairy tales children enjoy today were not written down until the seventeenth century. They had been told and retold, word for word, over many generations.

After the invention of writing, literature could be recorded permanently. A writing system could record the sounds of language, and create a communication system that would last longer than the life of any person. The first writing systems were devised about 3000 B.C. in the Middle East. The alphabet—a system of letters representing sounds—came later, in about 2000 B.C. Alphabets existed in various forms in the ancient world. The ancestor of the English, and most other European alphabets, is the Greek alphabet, known from the eighth century B.C. Other important alphabets include Arabic, Hebrew, Hindi, Persian, and Russian. Chinese and Japanese are written in ideographic or picture-sign scripts. Some of the earliest known writing remains unread because we no longer know how to unlock the meaning of the signs and symbols.

Creative writing

How did creative writing develop? The oldest writings are records that have a practical purpose—lists of rulers, family trees, records of battles, even notes of the year's business in a royal granary. To have any use, such records had to be made permanent by being written on a long-lasting material such as a stone wall, a clay tablet, or a parchment made of animal skin. Songs, stories, and tales to amuse and frighten children were forms of oral literature that were not written down because everyone knew them by heart. Creative writing began to develop as civilization advanced, allowing the wealthy (kings and other rulers) both the power and the leisure to enjoy the pleasures of literature. Among the court entertainers of Assyria, Babylon, Egypt, and China there appeared a new figure, the poet and bard. He would sing or recite in praise of the king (as David praised King Saul in the Bible), bring news of famous victories, or lament death and defeat. These compositions could be written down for the generations that followed, as a mark of the ruler's greatness.

Myths and legends, which were told for many generations and retained ancient folk-memories, became part of national epics. Homer's *Iliad*, for example, is an ancient Greek epic poem recounting events of the Trojan War. Myths common to many world literatures described the creation of the world; such stories became the foundations of a nation's writing. Eventually, oral and written literatures combined: in Europe, the stories told by minstrels about folk-heroes such as King Arthur and Robin Hood passed into written literature, to be retold for each new generation. The way in which oral tradition can preserve a cultural heritage has been demonstrated in modern times, as, for example, the American writer Maxine Hong Kingston found in the tales of her ancestors the key to her heritage in China. She told her story in her book *The Woman Warrior*.

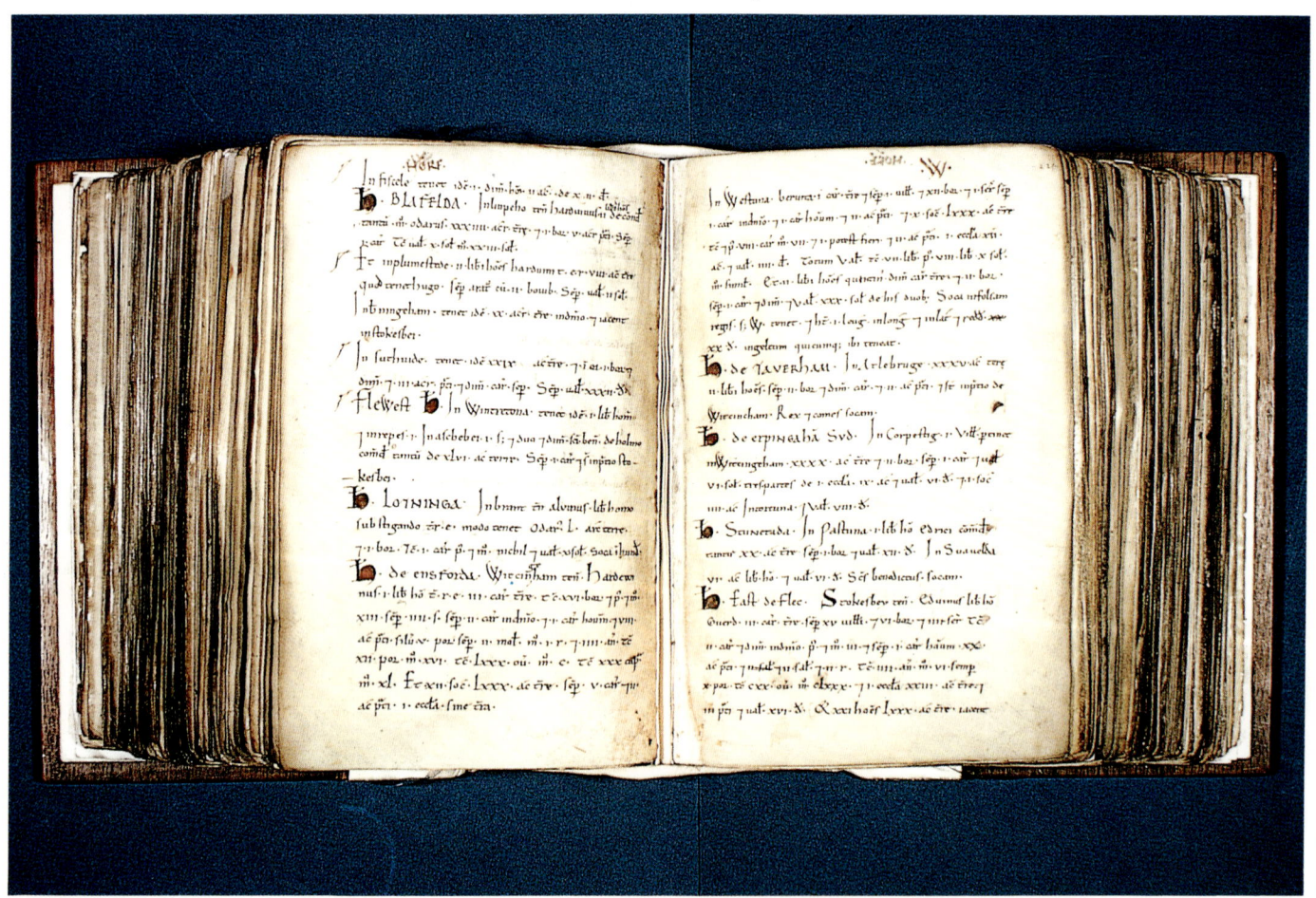

Above *Domesday Book is a unique record of England in 1086, compiled by Norman officials for William the Conqueror. The book lists towns and villages, their inhabitants, homes, lands and livestock, giving the king (and later historians) a written description of the kingdom the Normans had won by force of arms.*

The uses of literature

The Greek philosopher Aristotle concluded that literature, like all the arts, was imitation of life. The gods created; writers imitated. Poetry, he thought, was more valuable than history because it dealt with generalities—life, death, love, hate—whereas history confined itself to the doings of particular people at particular times.

This view was put forward almost 2,500 years ago, and people have argued about the "uses" of literature ever since. Most critics have agreed that literature is an invaluable record, and that without it civilization would have advanced far more slowly, if at all. From the earliest forms of "literature as record"—lists of kings, battles, and so on—the writing of history and of biography developed. Scientific writing is another form of literature as record, as are diaries and letters, and journalism. Such literature does more than merely record facts because the writers also comment and give an opinion; they then become commentators on events. James Boswell's biography (1791) of his friend and mentor Samuel Johnson is more than just a day-by-day account of the great man's doings and sayings: it is a record brought alive with comment and character. So, too, are the diaries written in seventeenth-century England by John Evelyn and Samuel Pepys; here again record is charged with additional interest through the imagination and intelligent self-awareness of the writer. The Old Testament of the Bible, begun at least 3,000 years ago, is another good example of a literary record. Ancient Greek historians such as Thucydides were admired and imitated by Roman writers such as Tacitus. The Roman dictator Julius Caesar was one of the first soldier-politicians to write his own account of history. English history-writing begins with the ninth-century *Anglo-Saxon Chronicle*, inspired by King Alfred the Great, which recounts the history of the West Saxons and their wars against the Danes.

Another function of literature is to inform. Through reading we learn and extend our knowledge, taking advantage of the experience and discoveries made by others. We use the written word to pass on information: without it we would have to rely on memory alone, each generation handing on a long recitation of "local knowledge." Memory alone is unreliable. Literature that provides information includes textbooks, reference books, scientific papers, and encyclopedias. Encyclopedias have a long history and the best of them attempt to be impartial. Among the earliest was the *Natural History* of the Roman writer Pliny the Elder, which included articles on geography, medicine, and art as well as science. Another was the vast Chinese *Great Encyclopedia* of the fifteenth century. In contrast, didactic literature, or propaganda, sets out to communicate a specific message, philosophical, political, or religious perhaps, such as Plato's *Republic* (c.368 B.C.), Sir Thomas More's *Utopia* (1516), *Das Kapital* (1867) by Karl Marx, the founder of modern Communism, or the *Confessions* of St. Augustine (c.397).

A textbook may be dull and still be studied because there is no alternative, but no storyteller will hold an audience with a dull tale. To keep a reader's attention literature seeks to entertain. Some literature may achieve this and do nothing more—a detective novel, an amusing article in a magazine, a funny poem, or a farce on stage. But entertainment is a central aim of more serious literature, too. The books we read may arouse a variety of emotions—horror, laughter, sadness, delight—but they must not bore us, or we will probably not reach the last page. Knowing this, writers often disguise a moral lesson in the trappings of a light-hearted tale as did Aesop in his *Fables*.

Below *A giant in the land of Lilliput, Gulliver captures the rival fleet of Blefuscu. The illustration is from an 1860 edition of Jonathan Swift's classic satire* Gulliver's Travels, *1726.*

Jonathan Swift's *Gulliver's Travels* (1726) may be read as a children's story but it has a cutting satirical edge, too. This blend of laughter and morality is the basis for the fable and the allegory. Most fiction entertains, novels and short stories in particular. But the best fiction does much more.

Any piece of writing may record, inform, and entertain. The skill of the writer determines whether reading is more than just a passing pleasure. A paperback thriller bought to pass the time on a plane trip is not likely to alter our opinions. And many of the books displayed in our local bookshop will be disposable and short-lived.

The plays of Sophocles, the poetry of Chaucer, the work of Shakespeare, Boccaccio, Dante, the novels of Cervantes, Dickens, Tolstoy, Austen, Twain; all are acknowledged masterpieces that have stood the test of time because they say something to people of every age. Shakespeare and Dickens were hardworking professional writers. Shakespeare wrote a new play when his fellow actors needed one. Dickens wrote his novels in serial form, turning out episodes as quickly as a modern scriptwriter writes for a TV soap opera. That they could also write with such deep insight into human nature makes them great writers and their works great literature.

Above *The detective fiction of Agatha Christie reaches even wider audiences via films and television. In this film version of* Death on the Nile, *Peter Ustinov (center) played the Belgian detective Hercule Poirot.*

Inset *Books are highly valued in developing countries, where education is hard-won. Customers browse at an outdoor display of books in Lahore, Pakistan.*

2 The Growth of Western Literature

Much ancient literature has vanished, lost in time. However, four ancient civilizations—Egypt, Babylon, Greece, and Rome—have left behind traces of their literature. Scholars have deciphered dead languages in order to read them. For example, The Rosetta Stone, discovered in Egypt in 1799, provided the key to reading Egyptian hieroglyphics. Unlike music, painting, and sculpture, literature is national, rather than international. A book must be translated if it is to cross language boundaries. Nevertheless, the growth of literature has been marked by constant borrowings between writers, each leaving behind echoes for the next generation.

Below *The Rosetta Stone bears the same text written in hieroglyphics (top), demotic, a simpler Egyptian script (middle), and Greek (lower). Twenty-three years after the stone's discovery, a Frenchman named Champollian was able to decipher the mystery of Egyptian hieroglyphics, using the stone as the key.*

The ancient world

Western literature—European and American—developed from the literature of ancient Greece. The Greeks transformed the age-old traditions of story-telling and myth-making into literary forms still alive today: history, philosophy, epic and lyric verse, and drama. The greatest Greek poems, Homer's epics the *Iliad* and the *Odyssey*, have continued to influence writers ever since. Greek literature also included reference books on astronomy, medicine, mathematics, and grammar, and the Greeks enjoyed romances, which can claim to be the first novels written in Europe.

Above *Pilgrims on the road to Canterbury: such a collection of colorful characters provides the framework for Chaucer's brilliant telling of the* Canterbury Tales. *Written in the London dialect from which modern standard English developed, Chaucer's wise, great poem is easier to understand today than most medieval English poems.*

The Romans borrowed much from Greece, in poetry and drama. The golden age of Roman literature—between 70 B.C. and A.D. 20—spanned the last years of the Republic and the first years of the Empire. Poets of Rome include Lucretius, Ovid, Virgil, and Juvenal. Virgil's *Aeneid* was an epic poem; like Homer's *Iliad* it was concerned with the Trojan War and also with the foundation of Rome. The Romans loved oratory, and the finest speeches of Rome's greatest orators, such as Cicero, were in themselves literary masterpieces. Throughout the Roman Empire, Latin became the language of government, of the law, and of scholarship; for centuries after the fall of the Roman Empire in the fifth century A.D., record-keeping and history were in Latin, rather than in the various vernacular languages of Europe.

Rome, like Greece, developed a "national" consciousness through its literature. This happened in other cultures, too. The Persian poet Firdausi wrote an epic poem, *Shahnama*, which describes the legendary history of Persia in 60,000 couplets. Hindu India produced the *Ramayana* and the *Mahabharata*; Babylon the *Gilgamesh* epic; Spain the story of El Cid; Iceland the sagas of the northlands, and so on. The best-known Old English poem is *Beowulf* (written c. A.D. 1000) which combines the old heroic paganism with a new Christian tradition.

Medieval literature

The greatest of European literary heroes of the Middle Ages is King Arthur, closely followed by the Emperor Charlemagne. Charlemagne's deeds are related in the medieval French *chansons de gestes* (tales of heroic deeds). France was the home of the first Arthurian tales, written as "romances." There were similar tales about Alexander the Great and other famous heroes of the past, but the most influential were the adventures of Arthur and his fabled knights. Equally important was the influence of three great Italian writers of the fourteenth century: Dante, Petrarch, and Boccaccio.

Latin remained the shared language of European literature until the late Middle Ages. English writers did not use everyday English until the 1300s, when Geoffrey Chaucer's *Canterbury Tales* (c.1387) became a landmark in this use of the vernacular language. When Chaucer was writing, at the end of the fourteenth century, Italy was the center of a European cultural revolution known later as the Renaissance. Dante, Petrarch, and Boccaccio were its literary leaders, and they were read and imitated everywhere. This was also the age of exploration. By the end of the fifteenth century, Vasco da Gama had traveled to India, and Columbus to the Caribbean. It was an age that provided writers with many new ideas. The Portuguese poet Luis de Camões hailed the achievements of the Portuguese seafarers in *The Lusiads* (1572), an epic poem that is a highlight of Portuguese literature, and which is still studied today.

Equally stimulating was the Reformation. This is the name given to the split in the Christian Church between Catholic tradition and new Protestant radicalism in the early sixteenth century. Translating the

Left inset *Rama exiled in the forest, a scene from the* Ramayana. *One of the two great national poems of India, the work was written about 300 B.C. and is based on older oral tales.*

Below *Printing in the late 1400s. The man seated is composing (setting) type on a stick held in his right hand. His colleagues are printing paper sheets using a screw press. A flood of books, old and new, appeared at this time as printing presses were constructed all over Europe.*

Above *This portrait of William Shakespeare by Martin Droeshout appeared on the frontispiece of the first collected edition of his plays (1623). It is probably the closest likeness there is of the great playwright.*

Bible into different national languages was a symbol of this movement. Writers felt freer to explore new themes, although personal writing was rare; most authors produced work for a public audience and seldom revealed their own innermost feelings.

English literature after 1500

Drama and poetry flowered from the sixteenth century onward, especially in England, which produced in William Shakespeare the most renowned of all writers. There followed the political and religious turmoil of the Civil War (1642–48); the Restoration of the monarchy (1660), and with it the playhouse, banned by the Puritans; and in the early 1700s, the formal wit and often cruel satire of Dryden, Pope, and Swift.

In English literature, poetry had a new and vigorous rival in the novel, written not in verse but in prose. Finding themselves increasingly out of sympathy with society, poets demanded change, and at the same time became more unsure of their role. Seeking fresh inspiration in nature, their own imaginations, and the political promise of the French Revolution (1789) came a new generation of writers grouped together as "Romantics" (though they were very individualist in their ideas and work). Among them were Blake, Wordsworth, Coleridge, Keats, Shelley, and Byron. The writer himself (or herself) now became the center of literary concern.

The nineteenth century was very much the age of the British novel. The century opened with the social satire of Jane Austen, and among the other great British novelists were Charles Dickens, the Brontë sisters, William Makepeace Thackeray, and George Eliot (Mary Ann Evans). The novel's popularity was maintained at the end of the century by writers such as Thomas Hardy, Robert Louis Stevenson, and Rudyard Kipling.

By the nineteenth century English was no longer a language confined to the British Isles. It was also the language of American and Canadian literatures, of Australia and New Zealand, and of writers in India, Africa, and the Caribbean.

Right *A painting of the Brontë sisters by their brother Branwell. From left to right they are: Anne (1820–49), Emily (1818–48), and Charlotte (1816–55). The Brontës spent most of their lives at home, and writing provided the outlet for their imaginative powers.*

Right *Pictured the year before his death in 1832, Goethe, greatest of all Germany's Romantic writers, dictates to his secretary.*

European literature

The literatures of Spain and France developed vigorously from the sixteenth century on. Two of Europe's leading dramatists were the Spaniards Lope de Vega Carpio and Pedro Calderón. In France there were distinctive national writers in Francois Rabelais, the essayist Michel de Montaigne, and the poets known as the Pleiades (after the stars), of whom the greatest was Pierre de Ronsard.

France continued to be the leader of European literature through the seventeenth century, which produced the fables of Jean de La Fontaine, the philosophical writings of René Descartes, and the Neoclassical plays by Pierre Corneille and Jean Racine. The comedies of Jean-Baptiste Poquelin, better known as Molière, have stood the test of time well and are still much enjoyed.

France was also the center of eighteenth-century "reason and enlightenment," the outstanding names are those of Jean-Jacques Rousseau and Voltaire. The Romantic movement in Europe, a forceful reaction to the "Enlightenment," was strongest in Germany. Johann Wolfgang von Goethe and Johann Friedrich von Schiller were the leading German Romantics. In France, Romanticism in literature was inspired by the French Revolution (1789), and flowered in the poetry of writers such as Victor Hugo, Alfred de Musset, and Charles Baudelaire, whose collection *Les Fleurs du Mal* (Flowers of Evil, 1857) caused a public outcry; French writers developed the ideal of "art for art's sake," and also explored the use of symbolism and impressionistic imagery in poetry. Among the leading Symbolist writers were the poets Paul Verlaine, Arthur Rimbaud, and Stephane Mallarmé.

In prose writing, the French excelled in realism, Hugo's *Les Misérables*, for example, and romantic adventures, such as Alexandre Dumas's *Three Musketeers* (1844). The harsher aspect of life in a Europe being changed by industrial and social revolutions was depicted in the naturalistic fiction of Emile Zola. The nineteenth century saw a new outburst of creativity in Russia, through the writing of Aleksandr Pushkin, Nikolai Gogol, and the great novelists and short-story writers Fyodor Dostoevsky, Mikhail Lermontov, Ivan Turgenev, and Leo Tolstoy. Scandinavia gave the world two major, influential dramatists, the Swede August Strindberg and the Norwegian Henrik Ibsen.

It was in the nineteenth century that popular reading habits became established. Before that time, few ordinary people could read or write. Throughout the Middle Ages books had been scarce and precious. They had been written by hand by educated men (usually monks), and most were religious or historical in theme. After the 1400s, with the invention of the printing press, books became cheaper to produce.

Below *The Russian novelist Leo Tolstoy (1828–1910) at work in old age and (inset) British writer Iris Murdoch (b.1919). Most novelists attempt to explore moral issues through the experience of fictional events and characters. The best of their works survive the test of time, as have Tolstoy's* War and Peace *and* Anna Karenina. *Posterity will judge the work of contemporary novelists such as Iris Murdoch.*

Literature was no longer the exclusive property of the church, court, or university. Printers and booksellers developed their trades, and by the 1700s there was a growing demand for literature of many kinds: ballads, political pamphlets, journals, newspapers, novels, poems, works on science and technology. During the 1800s public libraries helped satisfy a new generation of eager readers, emerging from the slowly developing state school systems of Europe. Alongside the great novels of Dickens and Honoré de Balzac were hundreds of sensational and sentimental examples of popular fiction. Children's literature, too, was by now an art of its own.

The twentieth century has seen a vast outpouring of printed words—books, magazines, newspapers, periodicals, and scholarly papers of every kind. Amid this mass of information, many creative writers seemed in retreat from what they saw as a disordered society. The catastrophe of World War I (1914–18), with the appalling carnage of trench warfare, produced the bleak poetry of Wilfred Owen, Siegfried Sassoon, and others. After the war, there was a mood of regret for the past and pessimism about the future.

Leading European novelists of the early twentieth century included Joseph Conrad (Polish born) who became a master in the English language, D.H. Lawrence, Marcel Proust, E.M. Forster, and Virginia Woolf. It was clear that the novel tradition remained strong in the work of writers such as Graham Greene and Evelyn Waugh in the 1930s, and in the work of a lively post-World War II generation, among them Kingsley Amis, Anthony Burgess, William Golding, Iris Murdoch, and Margaret Drabble in Britain; Albert Camus and Alain Robbe-Grillet in France; Alberto Moravia and Italo Calvino in Italy; Günter Grass in Germany; Aleksandr Solzhenitsyn and Boris Pasternak in the Soviet Union.

American literature

In modern times the balance of power shifted, in literature as in military terms, from the Old World to the New. American literature had its origins in the seventeenth century, in the early Colonial period with the poetry of Anne Bradstreet and the historical writing of Cotton Mather. The revolutionary fervor leading to the War of Independence (1776–83) spawned much political writing and an original American voice, adapting European influences to the New World. The early nineteenth century produced impressive prose writing by authors such as Washington Irving, Edgar Allan Poe, and Nathaniel Hawthorne. The American literary establishment was created by Ralph Waldo Emerson, Henry David Thoreau, and others: its tone was optimistic and trusting to human insight to overcome all hurdles. Herman Melville's *Moby Dick* (1851) is one of the world's most powerful Symbolist novels. Walt Whitman pioneered a vibrant, energetic, American-sounding poetry. Kate Chopin's *The Awakening* (1899) aroused public outcry at the turn of the century, but is now recognized as a masterpiece of feminist literature.

Below *Melville's* Moby Dick *(1851) is one of the great American works of fiction. This 1926 illustration by Rowland Hilder shows the whaling ship* Pequod, *whose crew hunt for the great white whale,* Moby Dick.

Toward the end of the nineteenth century America's great humorous writer Mark Twain wrote about life on the Mississippi River, while Jack London wrote about the American wilderness. Henry James went to Europe, where he wrote novels analyzing the differences between Old and New Worlds.

During the next decades Upton Sinclair and Sinclair Lewis wrote about the small towns and booming business world in early twentieth-century America. Black writers began to make their mark; James Weldon Johnson, Leroi Jones, James Baldwin, Ralph Ellison, Gwendolyn Brooks, Alice Walker, Maya Angelou, and others helped to establish what is today a flourishing tradition of black writing in the United States.

The twentieth century has seen the emergence of a number of gifted novelists. Through the range of its "serious" fiction, the appeal of popular thriller writers such as Raymond Chandler, and Dashiel Hammett, and through its dominance in film and TV production, American writing has been a powerful influence throughout the present century.

3 Eastern Literature

Asian literature has a longer history than Western literature. China, for example, has a writing tradition lasting from the fifth century B.C. to the Maoist Cultural Revolution of 1965–68; Chinese writers have influenced their neighbors in Japan, Korea, and Vietnam. Chinese poetry is written for its appearance, as well as for its sound and sense, because Chinese characters are more pictorial than Western letters. Originally all Chinese poetry was sung to music and is typically short and to the point.

The golden age of Chinese literature was the T'ang period (A.D. 618–907). The works of 2,000 poets from this era have been preserved and many have been translated into English. The Chinese also enjoyed novels. *Monkey* (1592), by Wu Ch'eng-en, resembles an Asian version of John Bunyan's *Pilgrim's Progress*, with many lively episodes and an assortment of monsters.

Japan's literature dates from the seventh century A.D. and much of it was originally written in Chinese. The earliest works were national chronicles such as the *Ihonshoki*. Later came poetry and novels, such as the tenth-century *Tale of a Bamboo Cutter*, and the *Tale of Genji*, (c.1000) written by a woman, Murasaki Shikibu, about a famous warrior prince who is also a a great lover. Drama includes the *Noh* and *Kabuki* plays. The most famous Japanese poetic form is the brief *haiku*. The Japanese enjoyed impromptu verse-making. One seventeenth-century poet composed more than 23,000 verses within twenty-four hours, dictating too fast for the scribes to write.

Above *A Kabuki actor. For over three hundred years Kabuki theater has been popular in Japan. The stories are full of incident and high emotion. Kabuki, despite the lavish costume, began as "people's theater," often transferring real-life stories to the stage.*

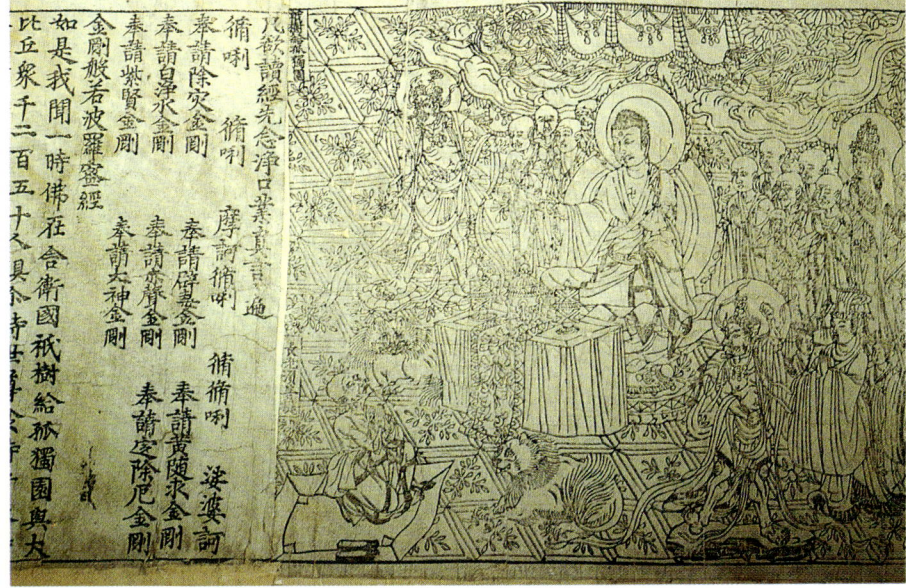

Left *The* Diamond Sutra, *one of the oldest printed books, was made in China in A.D. 868. Its seven paper sheets, printed from single carved wood blocks, are glued together to make a scroll.*

Indian literature was first written in Sanskrit and took as its themes the religious experiences of Hinduism. Folk tales, fables, and courtly romances were also popular and many found their way west to Arabia and Europe. Each language group of the Indian subcontinent has a rich literature. Tamil literature, for example, shows the influence of three religions—Buddhism, Hinduism, and most recently, Christianity. Particularly respected is Bengali literature, which includes epic poetry from the fourteenth century and works dedicated to the causes of social reform and Indian nationalism from the nineteenth century. The greatest single influence on Bengali literature was the poet Rabindranath Tagor (1861–1941). Hindi and Urdu literature flowered before the first contact with European culture in the seventeenth century, at the court of the Mogul emperors. Urdu has a link with Persian writing through the *ghazal*, a form of love poem that reached India from Persia.

Equally interesting are the literatures of Arabia. Before the Arabs adopted Islam (about A.D. 600) their poetry was intricate but exclusively oral. Written collections were not made until the eighth century. Classical Arabic, like ancient Greek and Latin, is a language that spans frontiers, and it was, and is, a powerful unifying force among Middle Eastern peoples. The golden age of Arabic literature was from A.D. 750 to 1200, when Arab writers were influenced by both Greek and Roman models. Equally strong was the tradition of the court poet. The Caliphs of Baghdad demanded tales still enjoyed today, such as *The Thousand and One Nights* with the adventures of Sindbad the Sailor. The *Rubáiyát* (c.1085) by the Persian poet Omar Khayyám was "reworked" into English by Edward FitzGerald in 1859.

4 Poetry

The English poet Samuel Taylor Coleridge defined poetry as "the best words in the best order." There have been many other definitions, attempting to summarize what makes poetry different from prose. Poetry is the literary form closest in effect to music, for it has rhythm (a regular beat) and is written in meter, that is, various arrangements of stressed and unstressed syllables. Poetry may also rhyme, using words that sound the same. Here is an example of rhyming verse from Ariel's song in Shakespeare's play *The Tempest*:

Full fathom five thy father *lies*;
Of his bones are coral *made*;
Those are pearls that were his *eyes*;
Nothing of him that doth *fade*
But doth suffer a sea-*change*
Into something rich and *strange*.

We can "scan," that is, mark the rhythm, or meter, of a line of verse, like this:

Fŭll fáth/ ŏm fíve/ thy fá/ thĕr liés/

Here the line has four pairs of stressed and unstressed sounds made up of words or syllables (parts of words). Each pair is known as a "foot," and in this example the meter is iambic. This means that each foot is made up of one unstressed sound followed by a stressed sound. If you say the line out loud you will hear the stressed pattern. A line of poetry may have as few as one foot, or as many as eight or more feet.

Apart from iambic, there are three other main kinds of meter: trochee (stressed, unstressed), anapest (unstressed, unstressed, stressed); and dactyl (stressed, unstressed, unstressed). One of the most popular forms in English verse is the iambic pentameter (pentameter = five feet in the line). This can be seen to its best effect in the rhymed "heroic" couplet verse of Alexander Pope and John Dryden, and also in the unrhymed blank verse of Shakespeare.

Much poetry is written in nonrhyming or blank verse. One of the most famous long poems written in blank verse is John Milton's *Paradise Lost* published in 1667. The poem describes the biblical Creation, and the temptation of humanity by the fallen angel, Satan. Here Milton describes Satan's flight toward his realm of Hell, and uses no end rhymes in his impressive blank verse:

Meanwhile the adversary of God and Man,
Satan, with thoughts inflam'd of highest design,
Puts on swift wings and towards the Gates of Hell
Explores his solitary flight . . .

Below *The poet John Milton (1608–74). After a brilliant youthful career, Milton determined to write an epic poem, overcoming personal disappointment and blindness (from about 1650) to achieve his aim in* Paradise Lost.

19

To Milton, rhyme was "the invention of a barbarous age," he regarded it as a "troublesome and modern bondage." Few poets today would attempt such a long epic poem as *Paradise Lost*. Nor are such works common to all literatures. The longest Chinese poem, for example, is seldom more than 100 lines, while the typical Japanese poem is even shorter. A long Japanese poem or *tanka* has thirty-one syllables; the more popular *haiku* has only seventeen. In such a condensed form, the poet strives to bring together thought and emotion in a striking image—such as a cherry blossom or a fish in a pool.

Poets use words descriptively, fashioning pictures in words through figures of speech, such as simile and metaphor. This is an example of a simple metaphor, from the nineteenth-century poet Alfred Noyes's work *The Highwayman*. The poet compares the moon to a sailing ship glimpsed on a wild night.

> The moon was a ghostly galleon tossed
> upon cloudy seas. . .

Poets delight in the magic of words, in making new associations between objects and images. John Keats's poem *On First Looking into Chapman's Homer* (1816) expresses the sensation of wonder felt by a poet encountering a new experience:

> Then felt I like some watcher of the skies
> When a new planet swims into his ken. . .

The poet uses words with the exuberance of some hearing them for the first time. This is Gerard Manley Hopkins, from his poem *The Windhover* (1877):

> I caught this morning morning's minion, kingdom
> of daylight's dauphin, dapple-dawn-drawn falcon.

William Shakespeare: Sonnet 18

Shall I compare thee to a summer's <u>day</u>?	A
Thou art more lovely and more tempe<u>rate</u>	B
Rough winds do shake the darling buds of <u>May</u>,	A
And summer's lease hath all too short a <u>date</u>;	B
Sometime too hot the eye of heaven <u>shines</u>,	C
And often is his gold complexion <u>dimm'd</u>;	D
And every fair from fair sometime de<u>clines</u>,	C
By chance of nature's changing course un<u>trimm'd</u>;	D
But thy eternal summer shall not <u>fade</u>,	E
Nor lose possession of that fair thou <u>owest</u>;	F
Nor shall death brag thous wander'st in his <u>shade</u>,	E
When in eternal lines to time thous <u>grow'st</u>	F
So long as men can breathe, or eyes can <u>see</u>,	G
So long lives this, and this gives life to <u>thee</u>.	G

John Milton: Sonnet 19 (on his blindness)

When I consider how my light is <u>spent</u>,	A
Ere half my days, in this dark world and <u>wide</u>,	B
And that one Talent which is death to <u>hide</u>,	B
Lodg'd with me useless, though my Soul more <u>bent</u>,	A
To serve therewith my Maker and pre<u>sent</u>	A
My true account, lest he returning <u>chide</u>,	B
Doth God exact day-labour, light de<u>ny'd</u>,	B
I fondly ask: But patience to pre<u>vent</u>	A
That murmur, soon replies, God doth not <u>need</u>	C
Either man's work or his own gifts, who <u>best</u>	D
Bear his mild yoke, they serve him best, his <u>State</u>	E
Is Kingly. Thousands at his bidding <u>speed</u>	C
And post o'er Land and Ocean without <u>rest</u>:	D
They also serve who only stand and <u>wait</u>.	E

Types of poetry

Poetry is often thought of as being concerned with private emotion, sometimes joyfully (a new love found), sometimes sad (an old love lost). Poets have written about every human experience from birth to death, about countryside and town, great events and small. Not all poetry is grave and serious; comic poetry often achieves a telling satirical effect by presenting a mundane subject in a mock-serious style. Alexander Pope, reflecting on the shortcomings of earthly justice, composed this barbed couplet:

> The hungry judges soon the sentence sign
> And wretches hang that jurymen may dine...

Narrative poems tell a story—Keats's *La Belle Dame Sans Merci* (1818) and Robert Browning's *The Pied Piper of Hamelin* (1842), for example, and Dylan Thomas's *Under Milk Wood* (a radio play for voices, 1954). Dramatic poetry may be part of a play. Shakespeare is the greatest dramatic poet in English, but modern poets such as T.S. Eliot have also written verse drama.

The lyric began as a sung poem in Greek and Roman times. It embraces such forms as the ballad, the ode, and the sonnet. Lyric poems are generally short and expressive, reflecting the innermost feelings of the poet. The French nineteenth-century poets Victor Hugo, Paul Verlaine, and Charles Baudelaire wrote fine lyric verse. So, too, did the Germans Goethe and Schiller, author of the *Ode to Joy* (1787). The twentieth-century American poets Marianne Moore and Robert Frost each wrote excellent lyric verse of very different styles. Odes may be addressed to a person or object. A famous example is Shelley's *Ode to the West Wind* (1819). An elegy is a poem written on the death of someone dear to the poet. Milton's *Lycidas* (1637) was written after the death of a friend. The American poet Walt Whitman's elegy *When Lilacs Last in the Dooryard Bloom'd* (1865–66) was written about the death of President Abraham Lincoln.

The sonnet (see box) is the nearest that Western literature comes to the compact, regular poetic forms that have for centuries been popular in the East. A sonnet always has fourteen lines, which may be rhymed in different ways. The sonnet form originated in Renaissance Italy, and in England developed into two distinct forms, largely through the sonnet writing of Shakespeare and Milton.

A history of poetry

The first English poet recorded in history is Caedmon, a monk of the seventh century. Caedmon wrote in Old English, and there is much to enjoy in the poetry of the Anglo-Saxons, whose literature ranges from riddles to story-poems such as the *Battle of Maldon* and the epic *Beowulf*. *Maldon* was the last great English poem before the Norman Conquest of 1066, when French language and literature began to shape the course of writing in English. Geoffrey Chaucer broke new ground in the fourteenth century by writing serious poetry in Middle English, when

Below *The poems and stories of Welsh writer Dylan Thomas (1914–55) display a delight in the sheer vibrancy of words. He is best known for his stories about growing up in Wales, and for the radio play* Under Milk Wood, *about a Welsh village. Thomas is pictured here (left) discussing the production of a radio broadcast with Ulster-born poet Louis MacNeice (1907–63).*

French and Latin were the languages of court and church. François Villon (1431–c.1470) breathed new life into French poetry, born of his experiences in the Paris underworld.

From the sixteenth century on national literatures were developing separate identities in Europe. Elsewhere, in India, Arabia, and China, for example, traditional forms continued. By the sixteenth century, the poets and dramatists of Elizabethan England were displaying an energy and exuberance that makes their work still fresh and engaging. The concept of "wit," clever and often baffling imagery, inspired the religious and love poems of John Donne and other so-called "metaphysical poets" of the early seventeenth century.

Alexander Pope declared that: "True wit is Nature to advantage dressed; what oft was thought, but ne'er so well expressed." In other words, the poet was the artist improving on nature, taking a general truth and giving it a distinctive quality through the workings of imagination and style. Pope and other European poets of the eighteenth-century Neoclassical school looked back to the cultures of Greece and Rome, sprinkling their poetry with references to Greek and Latin literature and mythology. As a reaction against this, the so-called Romantics of the later eighteenth and early nineteenth centuries looked for inspiration in Nature, the source of all truth, and in their fellow beings. William Wordsworth (1770–1850) was inspired by both the beauty of his native Cumbrian hills and by the promise of the French Revolution. But it was nature that remained the major source of poetic power:

My heart leaps up when I behold
A rainbow in the sky. . .

Above *Robert Burns (1759–96) is Scotland's national poet. Born poor, and educated by his father, Burn's talent earned the admiration of Edinburgh society, though his life was turbulent. He is best known for his beautiful songs and lyrics.*

Left *William Wordsworth's much-quoted poem beginning "I wandered lonely as a cloud" (1807) was inspired by a "host of golden daffodils" seen on a Lakeland (England) walk. The image, captured with what the poet called his "inward eye," became something never to be forgotten.*

Right *Emily Dickinson (1830–86) wrote for herself alone. Only two out of a thousand poems by her were published during her lifetime, and she lived as a virtual recluse.*

Above *The Brontë sisters spent most of their lives on the Yorkshire moors, at their father's Haworth parsonage. The wild, lonely landscape was a powerful influence in their writing.*

John Keats, Percy Bysshe Shelley, Lord Byron, and Emily Brontë, all writing in the early nineteenth century, were "second generation" English Romantics. All of them died young; Keats was only twenty-five when he died of tuberculosis, and his short, brilliant life helped to enlarge the myth of the poet as a "special" kind of artist. In Scotland, Robert Burns, whose use of local dialect reflected a growing interest in "nonpoetic" language, was destined to become a national, and international, institution.

The poets of the Victorian and modern eras often found themselves out of sympathy with the changes brought about by the industrial and social revolutions. The American Henry Thoreau (1817–62) ventured off into the woods to seek community in nature. Women poets such as Christina Rossetti and Elizabeth Barrett Browning enjoyed an increased respect. At the time of their first meeting, Elizabeth Barrett was regarded as a greater poet than her husband, Robert Browning. Her best work includes the "Sonnets from the Portuguese"—love poems written to her husband and published in 1844.

While the Brownings enjoyed the status of celebrities, other poets wrote in almost complete isolation from the world. America's greatest woman poet, Emily Dickinson, lived and wrote at home in Amherst, Massachusetts. She was practically unknown in literary circles and almost none of her poems were published until after her death in 1886.

The doubts and fears of the nineteenth-century poets seemed to be realized by the horrors of World War I (1914–18). A number of poets fought on the western front, and this generation (many of them, like Wilfred Owen, tragically short-lived) produced the greatest modern war poetry. After that war, poets in the United States and Europe seemed unsure of their role and followed a variety of paths, usually on uneasy terms with the world around them. T.S. Eliot saw the world as a wasteland; John Betjeman bemoaned the passing of a vanished England; Ted Hughes turned to nature; Ezra Pound, born in the American Midwest, took the whole world as his province. By mingling Chinese and Japanese influences with those of the Europeans, he demonstrated the unrivaled way in which poetry could experiment with new forms.

Today, poets are not usually public figures, as was Alfred, Lord Tennyson, who succeeded Wordsworth as England's Poet Laureate and was buried in Westminster Abbey in 1892. Yet poetry survives, and poetic language can be enjoyed not just on the printed page, but also in songs—through some pop music, for example. Today, poetry is truly international. Writers in North America and Europe read and are influenced by poets in other continents, such as the Chilean writer Pablo Neruda (1904–73), who dealt powerfully with contemporary social and political issues. In Neruda's case, a European language (Spanish) in a New World setting provides a rich creative medium for his message. This kind of cultural mix is a feature of modern literature, as the ancient literary traditions of Europe and Asia have been reshaped and reinvigorated in new settings. The United States, South America, Africa, and the Caribbean have all produced outstanding poets of the modern generation.

THE GENERAL.

'Good-morning; good-morning!' the General said
When we met him last week on our way to the Line.
Now the soldiers he smiled at are most of 'em dead,
And we're cursing his staff for incompetent swine.
'He's a cheery old card,' grunted Harry to Jack
As they slogged up to Arras with rifle and pack.
*   *   *
But he did for them both by his plan of attack.

Above *As a result of service in the trenches during World War I, Siegfried Sassoon wrote the poem, "The General" (1917). It is a brief but telling comment on the war's futility.*

Below *Battlefield horrors, far worse even than this 1916 scene of shell-blasted devastation on the Somme River, France, inspired Sassoon, Owen, Isaac Rosenberg, and other war poets, of whom only a few lived to see peace return.*

5 Prose

There are two main kinds of prose—storytelling, or fiction, and factual writing, or nonfiction. Prose is the "plain speech" of everyday life. Yet written prose developed after poetry. Prose differs from poetry in having neither set meter nor rhyme. Yet within the limits of sentences and paragraphs, the best prose has a rhythm and a music of its own, especially prose written to be spoken aloud. Prose writers aim for clear meaning, and so usually avoid the deliberate use of unfamiliar words or word arrangements. However, there are elaborate and experimental prose writers who write complicated text, just as there are obscure and "difficult" poets.

Prose fiction in English began in the Middle Ages. The poet Geoffrey Chaucer used prose when he translated foreign writers and also when he wrote about science, as in his account of the astrolabe, an instrument used for observing the stars. An early prose work was a religious book called *Revelations of Divine Love* (c.1393) by Juliana of Norwich. Sir Thomas Malory's tale of King Arthur, *Le Morte d'Arthur* (finished in 1470 and printed by William Caxton in 1485), was also written in prose. This was unusual because most imaginative writing had been in verse up to this time, chiefly because verse was easier for a minstrel to remember when singing or reciting. Prose had to be read: and there were very few books before the development of mechanical printing in the fifteenth century.

The novel
The novel, and to a lesser extent, the short story, are the major literary forms in prose. The novel is the youngest member of the literary family. It grew out of the medieval romance, a tale of chivalry and foreign adventure, heroism, and often grotesque humor. Giovanni Boccaccio's *The Decameron* (1349–51) retold old stories, and was itself widely copied. The word "novel" actually comes from Italian (*novella*), and in the sixteenth century Italian novels were rather popular in England— Shakespeare took the plot of his play *Othello* from one. In *Gargantua and Pantagruel* (1532–34) the French writer François Rabelais makes fun of the old romances, while Miguel Cervantes's *Don Quixote* (1605) is also mocking but takes a more serious tone. It was the first "great novel." It soon became obvious that the novel could teach as well as entertain. John Bunyan's *Pilgrim's Progress* (1678), a moral fable set in the framework of a traveler's tale, long remained one of the most widely read books in the English language.

Daniel Defoe was a prolific and versatile writer producing novels, pamphlets, and journals. His best-known work is *Robinson Crusoe* (1719)

Below *Cervantes's comic hero Don Quixote attempts to turn fiction into reality. Here he sets out on his knock-kneed nag to perform deeds of chivalry; reality trails behind, in the shape of his squire Sancho Panza. Cervantes's two-part novel (1605, 1615) is one of Europe's finest literary achievements.*

Above *This illustration by George Cruickshank c. 1887, is from Charles Dickens's* Oliver Twist. *The innocent Oliver is introduced by the Artful Dodger to Fagin, boss of the youthful pickpocket gang.*

which reads like a true-life account of a castaway; Defoe based his fiction on the true story of the marooned sailor Alexander Selkirk. Eighteenth-century novels contain a series of adventures of one hero crammed together within a loose plot, with frequent asides. They are known as "picaresque." A popular example is the hilarious *Tom Jones* (1749) by Henry Fielding. Other authors of the period, such as Samuel Richardson, Tobias Smollett, and Laurence Sterne, also helped to establish the novel's popularity, and the form developed rapidly. Women novelists, such as Eliza Haywood, were also popular. Her first novel, *Love in Excess*, was published in 1719. Jane Austen's six great novels are studies of character and psychology; her books have none of the harum-scarum incidents of the picaresque fictions. Instead they take a controlled, mocking, ironic look at English middle-class life.

The nineteenth-century adventure novels of Sir Walter Scott (Waverley novels c.1814–26) and later of Robert Louis Stevenson were much imitated: Stevenson's classic *Treasure Island* (1883) is as popular today as when it was written. Charles Dickens was perhaps the greatest of all English novelists. Memories of his boyhood inspired books such as *David Copperfield*, and his concern about the social ills of the time are expressed in *Oliver Twist* and *Hard Times*. Elizabeth Gaskell wrote novels about the hardship of the working class in Manchester, where she lived. George Eliot (the pseudonym of Mary Ann Evans (1810–80)) in such novels as *Middlemarch* (1872), and Anthony Trollope commented on contemporary society. From their isolated home on the Yorkshire moors, Charlotte, Emily, and Ann Brontë wrote novels of startling power.

Right *Jane Austen (1775–87) seldom traveled far from her Hampshire home. She began writing as a young girl, encouraged by her family, and wrote about the society she knew and understood. Her most popular novels are* Pride and Prejudice *and* Emma.

The nineteenth-century French writers Victor Hugo, Stendhal, Honoré de Balzac, Alexandre Dumas, Gustave Flaubert, and Emile Zola were leading figures in the growth of the novel. So, too, were the Russian writers of the period: Leo Tolstoy—whose famous *War and Peace* was published in 1869—and Fyodor Dostoevsky, Nikolai Gogol, and Ivan Turgenev.

Alongside the serious novel other branches of prose were thriving. From the Gothic thriller—Ann Radcliffe's *The Mysteries of Udolpho* (1794), Matthew Lewis's *The Monk* (1795), and Mary Shelley's *Frankenstein* (1818), for instance—the horror novel developed. This genre was later made famous by Edgar Allan Poe and Bram Stoker, the creator of Count Dracula. The ingenious Wilkie Collins pioneered the detective story, a form given even greater popularity by Sir Arthur Conan Doyle's later nineteenth-century creation of Sherlock Holmes, fiction's most famous detective. Modern detective story writers and

Above *An illustration by N.C. Wyeth shows the rascally pirate Long John Silver and young Jim Hawkins, his innocent victim, characters from Robert Louis Stevenson's* Treasure Island, *first published in 1883.*

Conan Doyle Uniform Edition

THE HOUND OF THE BASKERVILLES

Left The Hound of the Baskervilles *(1902) has attracted more lurid treatments (in illustration and on film) than most of Conan Doyle's stories. The author grew weary of his creation, Sherlock Holmes, and tried to kill off the famous detective. But the public outcry was such that Holmes was eventually resurrected!*

their renowned detectives include Agatha Christie (Hercule Poirot and Miss Marple), George Simenon (Inspector Maigret), Raymond Chandler (Philip Marlowe), P.D. James (Adam Dalgliesh), and others. Science fiction began with Jules Verne (*Five Weeks in a Balloon*, 1862), progressed by way of H.G. Wells (*The Time Machine*, 1895), Aldous Huxley (*Brave New World*, 1932), and now attracts some of the most imaginative modern writers. Comedy writing has produced such varied talents as Jerome K. Jerome (*Three Men in a Boat*, 1889), P.G. Wodehouse ("Jeeves" novels, from 1917), Joseph Heller (*Catch 22*, 1955), and John Irving (*The World According to Garp*, 1978).

The nineteenth century was the great age of the novel; the public was eager to read new works (often published as magazine serials) and the novelist was an important figure. Today the novel explores more areas of experience, including women's lives, experiences of minority peoples, and new social and sexual issues. Plot and character may no longer be the two central pillars of the novel. Writers have experimented with new methods, abandoning the "real" sequence of events, for a "stream of consciousness" technique, which can be difficult to understand. An important writer using this technique was the French novelist Marcel Proust whose *Remembrance of Things Past* (1913) is a lengthy and somewhat haphazard exploration of a person's mind. The Irish writer James Joyce used the same technique in his masterpiece, *Ulysses*, first published in Paris in 1922. Titles, too, give a hint of the modern mood: *The Trial* by Franz Kafka (1925); *The Rebel* by Albert Camus (1951); *A Room of One's Own* by Virginia Woolf (1929); *A Burnt-Out Case* by Graham Greene (1961).

Right *In* The War of the Worlds, *first published as a magazine serial in 1897, H.G. Wells envisaged a Martian invasion of the Earth. In the 1950s film version, from which this still is taken, the Martians chose to land in Grovers Mill, New Jersey.*

Left *Another corpse for Philip Marlowe, Raymond Chandler's laconic, world-weary private eye—here portrayed by Dick Powell in a 1940s movie of* Farewell My Lovely.

Below *Two leading American writers of the twentieth century were Ernest Hemingway (1899–1961), seen here in his library; and F. Scott Fitzgerald (1896–1926). Fitzgerald's novel* The Great Gatsby *(1925) describes the exuberance, yet moral emptiness, of the 1920s "Jazz Age"—here (lower) recreated on film.*

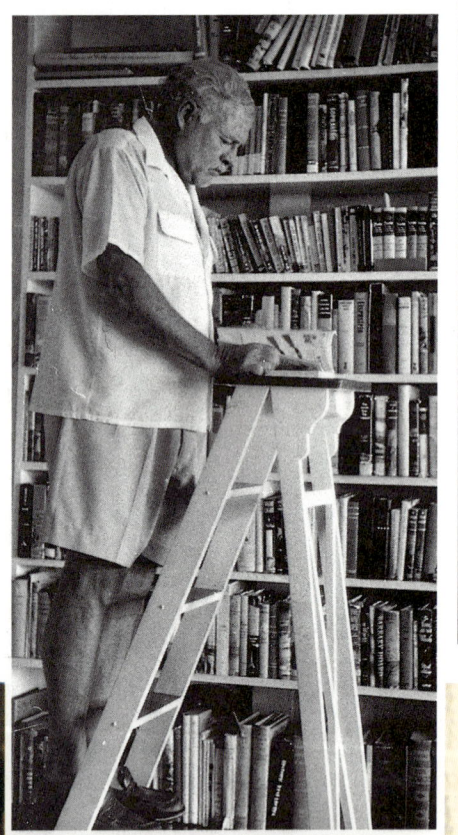

Novelists of the present century have written about the problems of the individual in a fast-changing, often uncaring world. Many have been critical of society. D.H. Lawrence saw a mechanical brutishness threatening human relationships; Evelyn Waugh found much of human behavior ridiculous, for instance in *Decline and Fall* (1928); and George Orwell foresaw new dictatorships. Many of the leading twentieth-century novelists have been American: notably Ernest Hemingway, William Faulkner, F. Scott Fitzgerald, James Baldwin, and Canadian-born Saul Bellow.

The novel has found fresh vitality in Africa, through writers such as the South Africans Alan Paton and André Brink, the Kenyan James Ngugi, and the Nigerians Chinua Achebe and Amos Tutuola. From the Caribbean and Latin America has come an impressive range of modern novel and short-story writing, from authors including Wilson Harris and V.S. Naipaul (West Indies), Jorge Amado (Brazil), Carlos Fuentes (Mexico), and Gabriel Garcia Marquez (Colombia).

A number of novelists have also excelled at writing short stories, a form that can be traced back to the fables and tales of Arabia, and to the popular romances of the Middle Ages. The fables of Aesop (sixth century B.C.), who is thought to have been a Greek slave, and of Jean de La Fontaine in the seventeenth century, were short stories making a moral point. The Brer Rabbit stories of the American author Joel Chandler Harris are similar, merging African traditional tales into an American setting.

Early novels often included separate short stories, as digressions from the main plot. Masters of the short-story form include Edgar Allan

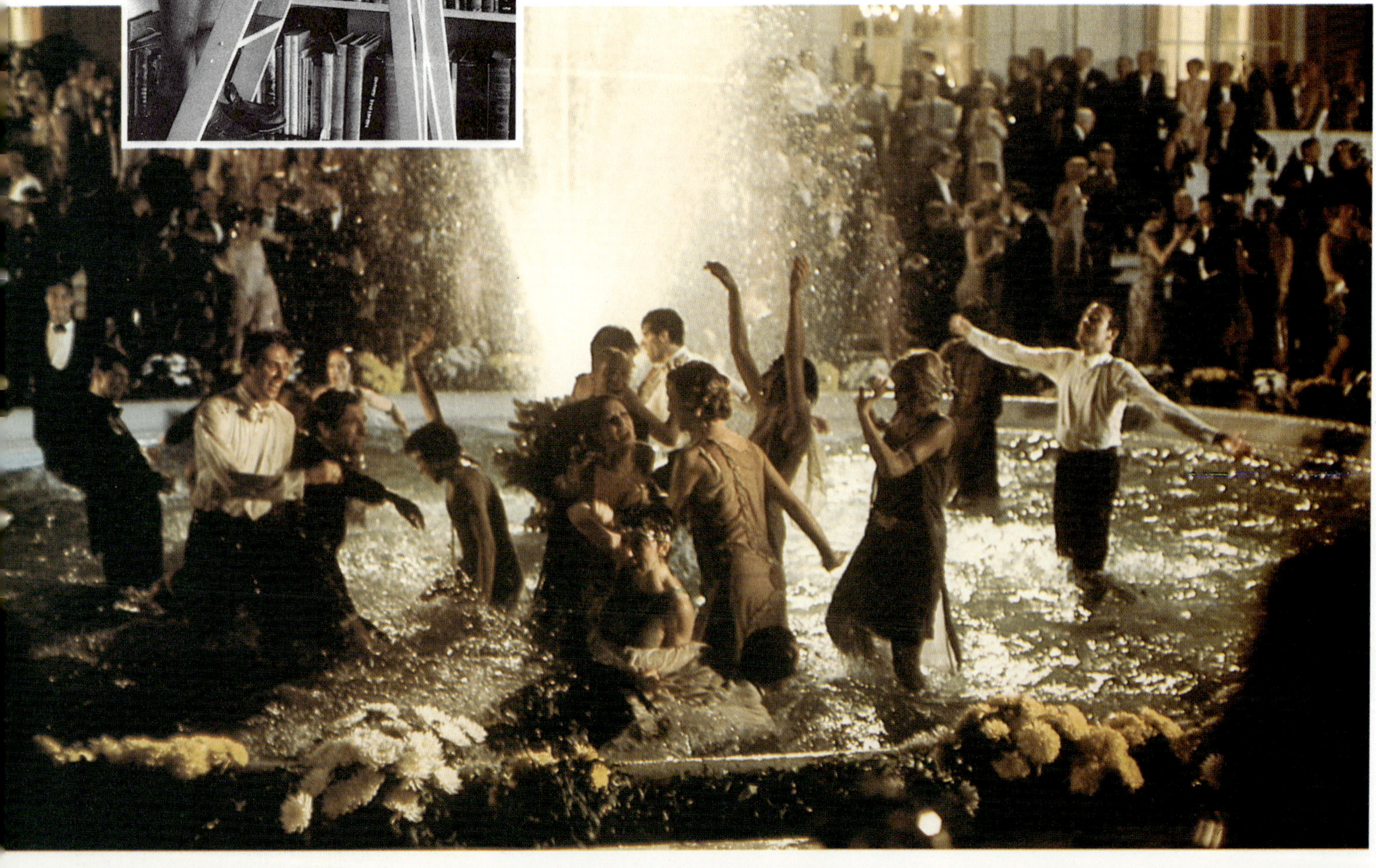

Poe, Katherine Mansfield, James Joyce, Guy de Maupassant, Jean Rhys, Somerset Maugham, Colette, and Graham Greene. Mark Twain, O. Henry, and James Thurber added a distinctive American humor to the short story, while M.R. James was a master of the ghost story. Many science fiction writers have also chosen to write short stories, often published in magazines rather than in books.

Nonfiction prose

Prose has long been used to supply information; writing in the sixteenth century, Sir Francis Bacon is famous for his essays, as well as for his writings on politics and science. Thomas Browne, who studied medicine, wrote rich prose in a colorful style on a wide range of subjects including human and natural history. The 1600s saw the work of Isaak Walton, author of *The Compleat Angler* (1653), and the diaries of John Evelyn and Samuel Pepys. The first newspapers appeared, and with them a new profession: journalism. In England Richard Steele and Joseph Addison created *The Tatler* (first issue 1709) and *The Spectator* (first issue 1711), the most-read magazines of the day. There was much political comment, often biting, and writings on religious and philosophical matters. Memoirs and letters give us an insight into life in the eighteenth and nineteenth centuries. The publication of Dr. Johnson's *Dictionary* in 1755 was a landmark in scholarship. Johnson was also one of the first English literary critics, and produced an edition of Shakespeare's plays with critical notes. In 1709 the first Copyright Act became law in England, giving authors a fair share in the profits of their work; previously all books had been the property of the printer.

Prose writing reached new heights in the eighteenth and nineteenth centuries with works by historians such as Edward Gibbon and Thomas Macaulay; in economics and politics through the writings of Edmund Burke, Thomas Paine, Adam Smith, and William Cobbett; and in natural history through the work of Gilbert White. The Industrial Revolution and the rapid growth of technology gave rise to a vast new technical literature, ranging from papers by the scientist Michael Faraday to Charles Darwin's *On the Origin of Species* (1859).

Poetry had now become largely a private communication between poet and reader, whereas prose was addressed to the world at large. Prose propaganda has remained a powerful influence; almost everyone with a case to argue, from Karl Marx to Adolf Hitler, from Mahatma Gandhi to Germaine Greer, has written a book setting out his or her personal views and opinions.

Travel writing, sports reporting, biography, cookbooks, magazine articles for every conceivable interest, political and social commentary—the spectrum of interests covered by prose writing today is enormous. Most of what we read is prose, ranging from the caption of a news photograph to a leading article in a paper, from a paperback bought at a drugstore to a textbook. After its slow beginnings, prose has become literature's most formidable force.

Below *Karl Marx (1818–83) was a revolutionary through writing, not fighting. The founder of modern Communism spent many years as an exile in London, working in the Reading Room of the British Museum. His major works are the* Communist Manifesto *(with Engels, 1848) and* Das Kapital *(1867, with further volumes 1885, 1894).*

6 Drama

Drama is literature acted out—often in words, sometimes with music and other extras such as scenery, costume, lighting, and sound effects. It may be played on a stage in front of a "live" audience, or in a broadcasting or film studio. Film, radio, and television need a technological "stage" for drama to be enacted and transmitted, but live actors can perform anywhere.

The beginnings of drama

Drama evolved long ago from religious rituals involving music, song, and dance. Through drama people acted out familiar stories, the deeds of gods, and the behavior of humans and animals. Much early drama was composed in verse and very little was actually written down. Western drama has its roots in ancient Greece where, 2,500 years ago, actors wearing masks performed plays written by Aeschylus, Sophocles, and Euripides. These were the three masters of tragedy, who told stories in which heroes were laid low by fate and by their own moral weaknesses. The greatest Greek comedy writer was Aristophanes, who ridiculed the pompous and the mighty.

The masks worn by Greek actors were large enough to be seen easily by an audience sitting in tiers around an open-air stage. The mask identified the character played by each actor; a change of mask meant that a new character had appeared. The dramatist had to persuade the audience to accept the rules of the play, knowing that the audience was aware that the play was not "real." Little scenery was needed.

The chorus was a vital element of the Greek drama, commenting on the action and providing both a link between characters and audience, and at times a voice for the dramatist. In Shakespeare's day, it was enough for an actor, as chorus, to begin a play with an appeal to the audience's imagination. *Henry V* opens with the chorus:

"Suppose within the girdle of these walls
Are now confined two mighty monarchies...
... piece out our imperfections with your thoughts."

In modern drama, the writer relies more on the characters themselves to convey any argument. Occasionally, characters reveal themselves directly through soliloquies, speaking either to themselves or to the audience.

The Roman theater borrowed much from the Greeks, but Roman plays lacked the timeless quality of the greatest Greek drama. Indeed, toward the end of the Roman Empire plays became so crude and vulgar that they aroused hostility from the emerging Christian church, and

Right *Masked actors perform the* Oresteia *by Aeschylus (525–465 B.C.), first of the great Greek dramatists. The three-play cycle tells of the tragedies that befall the family of King Agamemnon. (Orestes is the king's son.)*

this led to the loss of professional theater in Europe throughout most of the Middle Ages. Despite this, the same church sponsored the drama that remained. This included the miracle, mystery, and morality plays that retold stories from the Bible, and simple moral fables in which stock characters—vices, virtues, fools, St. George, the Devil—appeared again and again.

Drama took on fresh vigor in the sixteenth century in Italy, where the *Commedia dell'Arte* relied heavily on improvisation. Professional players, mostly masked, were free to elaborate on a basic plot. In England, drama flourished during the late sixteenth and early seventeenth centuries. The leading writer was William Shakespeare but there were many other writers whose plays were popular, including Thomas Kyd, Christopher Marlowe, Ben Jonson, Francis Beaumont, John Fletcher, John Webster, and John Ford. The actors were all men (women's parts were played by boys); they formed companies, built theaters, and employed professional writers.

Mr Elle... as Harlequin. (Second Position.) № 30.

Right *An eighteenth-century actor as Harlequin. In the Italian Commedia dell'Arte, the character of Harelquin (Arlechino) was a quick-witted servant. In English pantomine, he became an elegant mute, vying with the Clown for the love of Columbine. Arlechino's comic "slapstick" has become Harlequin's magic wand.*

34

Shakespeare's plots were mostly borrowed, but he lifted them to rare heights through the power of his verse and the range of his imaginative vision. He wrote history plays about the ancient and recent past such as *Titus Andronicus* and *Henry V*; comedies about love and human relations—*A Midsummer Night's Dream* and *Romeo and Juliet*, for example; and tragedies, including *Hamlet, Othello, King Lear, Antony and Cleopatra,* and *Macbeth*. Few dispute Shakespeare's position as the greatest dramatist who has ever lived.

Shakespeare's art was a profession. He was an actor himself, and he wrote at least thirty-six plays between 1589 and 1613. The so-called First Folio edition of these plays was not published until 1623, seven years after his death. It was not until the eighteenth and nineteenth centuries that the "Shakespeare industry" began to grow. No other author in the world has been so much studied or written about. Fortunately, his plays are also still performed, and enjoyed, every generation finding in them new challenges and inspiration.

Top *Rosalind (disguised as a boy) and Orlando in a scene from a Royal Shakespeare Company production of Shakespeare's* As You Like It *(written about 1599).* **Inset** *A bleaker Shakespearean vision: Laurence Olivier as the king in the tragedy* King Lear *(written about 1605).*

Restoration drama and after

After Shakespeare, English theater at first subsided into bloodthirsty melodrama and was eventually banned altogether by the Puritans. With the Restoration of King Charles II in 1660 English theater returned to present a new form of play, the comedy of manners, such as those of William Wycherley, William Congreve, Aphra Behn, and Sir George Etherege. Restoration comedy's blend of social satire, family misunderstanding, convoluted plot, and confused love-lives remains enjoyable, and taps a rich vein still being exploited by dramatists. In the late 1700s Richard Brinsley Sheridan dominated English theater with his brilliant comedies.

In France the great comedy writer was Molière. Other French dramatists of this period, such as Jean Racine, chose to follow formal classical models. The freer, more spontaneous roots of the British theater allowed it to develop even during the nineteenth century when, although great actors emerged, great new plays did not.

Toward the close of the nineteenth century, Realism and Naturalism came to the stage. Writers such as George Bernard Shaw, Anton Chekhov, Henrik Ibsen, and August Strindberg tackled contemporary social issues frankly and in the language of everyday speech. The arrival of the cinema and television in the twentieth century has completed this emancipation. A playwright may now begin the story at the end of the time-sequence, and range back and forth within it—a technique that would have horrified the ancient Greeks. Modern dramatists, such as Eugene O'Neill, Samuel Beckett, Arthur Miller, and Harold Pinter, have explored many aspects of human experience, concentrating on the psychology of the individual and the tensions in relationships. In addition to the theater, the movies and television now provide new outlets for dramatic writing.

36

Modern dramatic media

Writing for stage and screen is not the same as writing a novel. A novel is a physical arrangement of words on a page; the writer controls each word, and knows that only the reader can "interfere" with them. A screen or stage-play is not the sole property of the author. Inevitably, it will change in the hands of actors, director, camera crew, and film editor. The author knows that every performance of a stage or television play or film will be different, and the audience may be influenced much more by what they see than by the words they hear.

The struggling novelist or poet perhaps has fewer problems than the would-be playwright, striving to have a play performed. Putting on a play is a long and costly business. It is no good writing a play that is set during the French Revolution and demands a cast of fifty actors plus several hundred extras for the big scenes, and expect it to be taken on by a local repertory group. Fringe theater and small low-cost actors' companies offer opportunities for new plays, mostly small-scale, to be performed. Otherwise, the writer must seek a patron, just as in Shakespeare's day. Today, a group of business people, or backers, rather than an aristocrat, may provide such patronage. The Abbey Theatre, Dublin, provided a staging for leading Irish dramatists of the early twentieth century. Many American writers and actors get a start in "off-Broadway" productions or repertory company productions in theaters throughout the country. The British National Theatre has put on new plays by dramatists such as David Hare and Howard Brenton, both of whom originated in fringe theater. Writing radio plays has given a number of young writers their first breakthrough and encouragement. Radio allows the dramatist a unique freedom to use language to capture the concentration and imagination of an audience.

A number of leading modern dramatists, Dennis Potter, for example, write more for television than for the stage, creating dramas in which visual images, music, and camera technique have as much impact as the words spoken by the actors.

Below *Actors broadcasting a radio drama. Writing for radio, where listeners create their own visual impressions, demands special skills. A number of modern writers have turned to radio, television, and film.*

7 Literature and Society

Writers of all periods have questioned society's values and sought fresh answers. At times, in Shakespeare's day, for example, writers have enjoyed patronage from the rich and powerful, but such patronage has not stifled the critical voices of the best among them. Two thousand years ago, Aristophanes mocked the Greek establishment and the follies of the human race, while more recently, most people would agree that no satire has been more devastating than George Orwell's *Animal Farm*, written in 1946.

Politics and literature

The revolutionary writer emerged in the late eighteenth century, as the Romantic movement found itself at odds with the onward march of the Industrial Revolution. Both the American Revolution (1776) and the French Revolution (1789) owed much of their inspiration to the writings of radical thinkers such as Jean-Jacques Rousseau and Thomas Paine.

The novels of Charles Dickens helped to make people more aware of the plight of the poor in nineteenth-century Britain. In the United States *Uncle Tom's Cabin* (1850) by Harriet Beecher Stowe stirred many Americans to an awareness of the evils of slavery in the southern states. The book sold half a million copies and was translated into twenty-two foreign languages. Though later regarded with mixed feelings by many black Americans, *Uncle Tom's Cabin* demonstrated the power of books to influence public opinion.

Above *Thomas Paine (1737–1809) was a radical who supported both the American and French Revolutions. His pamphlets and books on the theme of the "Rights of Man" greatly influenced Americans in their fight for independence (1775–83) and the revolutionaries in France.*

Left *Black slaves in Washington, D.C., 1819. Books and newspapers helped to arouse public indignation at the plight of slaves and played an important part in bringing about the abolition of slavery in the United States.*

A black writer named Phillis Wheatley (b.1753) was the second woman poet to have her poems published in America, and the first black woman to do so. Women writers had to struggle long and hard for recognition, although a few individuals such as the playwright Aphra Behn succeeded in a predominantly male world. Aphra Behn (b.1640) was the most famous woman writer in England before the nineteenth century. The achievement of Jane Austen, the Brontë sisters, George Eliot, George Sand (Armandine-Aurore Lucille Dupin), Elizabeth Barrett Browning, Christina Rossetti, and others, helped to establish women's place in literature.

Women writers secured a place of gradually increasing significance in the early twentieth century—though the "victory" was hard-won. Virginia Woolf, one of the "Bloomsbury group" of London-based modernists, describes in *A Room of One's Own* (1929) the particular challenge of being a female writer in a male-dominated world.

In the later twentieth century writers such as Simone de Beauvoir (*The Second Sex*), Betty Friedan (*The Feminine Mystique*), Germaine Greer (*The Female Eunuch*), and Doris Lessing (*The Golden Notebook*) brought the issues central to the "women's movement" to the attention of a wide range of readers, both female and male. Feminist publishers have actively promoted women's writing.

Writers have often sought to give society a lead. Shaw's play *Pygmalion* (the model for the musical *My Fair Lady*) is a comedy of ideas, with a serious argument. John Galsworthy's play *Strife* (1900) was one of the first to deal realistically with industrial conflict. The American Clifford Odets wrote a play, *Waiting for Lefty* (1935), about a New York cab drivers' strike. John Steinbeck won a Pulitzer Prize for *The Grapes of Wrath* (1939), which brought the tragedy of the dust-bowl refugees of the United States in the 1930s to worldwide attention. In the 1950s the so-called angry young men, John Osborne, Arnold Wesker, and others, were critical of the state of Britain and the British theater. *Cry the*

Above *John Steinbeck's novel* The Grapes of Wrath *tells of the struggles of American migrant farmers in the Depression years of the 1930s. The book had considerable impact on public opinion.*

Below *Virginia Woolf, at the age of twenty (1902). In her novels she experimented with form, and in her* Writer's Diary *she recorded the development of each of her books. One of the so-called "Bloomsbury group" of writers and artists, she committed suicide in 1941.*

Beloved Country (1948) by Alan Paton stirred awareness about the racial tragedy looming in South Africa. Rachel Carson's *Silent Spring* (1962) was one of the first books to warn of environmental dangers from the uncontrolled use of chemical pesticides.

In his novel *1984* (1949) George Orwell foresaw a world in which the State controlled not only literature but thought itself. A tyrannical government may threaten both a writer's freedom to publish and personal liberty. Writers have braved much and suffered greatly in opposing repressive regimes—in Nazi Germany in the 1930s, in the Soviet Union under Stalin, in China during the worst excesses of the Cultural Revolution, and in South Africa under the apartheid regime. Writers refusing to "toe the party line" have risked isolation, imprisonment, exile, even death. Literature can become a focal point of opposition, through underground magazines and newsletters, and in books smuggled abroad for publication.

The Russian writer Aleksandr Solzhenitsyn in *The Gulag Archipelago* (first published in English in 1973) gives a chilling account of the experience of writers and others subjected to imprisonment under the Stalinist dictatorship. "In this book there are no fictitious persons, nor fictitious events . . . " he wrote. Russian writers had been divided by the 1917 Communist Revolution; many were enthusiastic revolutionaries; others foresaw continued dictatorship and oppression. Maxim Gorky,

at first hostile, later became a literary advisor to Stalin, dictator of the Soviet Union from 1924 to 1953, and an architect of the philosophy of socialist realism. Any book, play, poem, painting, or piece of music was judged by its value, or lack of it, to the onward march of communism. Works that were judged to lack the "correct" qualities were banned—as was Boris Pasternak's novel *Doctor Zhivago* (first published in Italy in 1957)—until the advent of Gorbachev-style *glasnost*, or "openness," in the 1980s. Isaac Babel, a Soviet Jewish writer, saw and described horrific atrocities in Russia; his work was attacked for being too "naturalistic" and was not published after 1937. Babel was arrested and in 1941 he died in a Soviet concentration camp.

Today, writers' freedom is regarded as a central plank of democracy, but even in a democracy, writers can suddenly find themselves under attack. This happened in the United States in the late 1940s and early 1950s, during the "McCarthy era" (so-named after Senator Joseph McCarthy who led a modern-day "witch-hunt"). Writers alleged to hold pro-Communist views—particularly those working in the Hollywood movie industry—were accused of "un-American activity" and had their careers ruined even if the allegations were untrue.

The status of literature

George Orwell would perhaps be pleasantly surprised today at the continuing readership of his own books, since during the 1940s he predicted gloomily that television would undoubtedly replace books and newspapers as people's main source of information. From what he observed of popular reading habits, he concluded that most people felt little need for literature, preferring to spend their money on other "recreations."

Writers, and not just writers of over-hyped bestsellers, do still enjoy a certain public fame. The major international literary award is the Nobel Prize for Literature, given each year to a writer for a life's work, rather than for a single book. It has been given to a number of famous writers in the past, including Rudyard Kipling, Rabindranath Tagore, W.B. Yeats, and George Bernard Shaw. In recent years the winners have included Patrick White, an Australian novelist (1973), Saul Bellow, an American novelist (1976), William Golding, a British novelist (1983), and Wole Soyinka, a Nigerian dramatist (1986).

Despite media interest in such awards, few writers today can claim to be household names. Some popular authors can earn enough from their books, mostly from selling the rights to make a movie or a TV serial, to sit back and enjoy the life style of a millionaire. But most live modestly. Modern writers rely on publishers to produce and sell their books. Many publishers today are part of large, often international, companies. A writer may still retain a personal relationship with a publisher, usually through an editor, but publishing is very much a business. It is hard for a first-time novelist to get a book published; little money is made from hardback fiction and most publishers prefer to play it safe with established authors.

Above *American playwright Arthur Miller (b.1915), whose best-known play is* Death of a Salesman *(1949). The play tells how a traveling salesman, Willy Loman, is destroyed by society's materialistic pressures. Another of his plays,* The Crucible *(1953), is about the appalling witch trials of the seventeenth century in Salem, Massachusetts. This is also a powerful response to the McCarthy "witch-hunts" of the 1950s, from which Miller himself suffered.*

Above *Nigerian writer Wole Soyinka (b.1934), in Sweden for the award of the 1986 Nobel Prize for Literature. The award drew attention to the considerable achievements of modern African writing.*

Today, English-language publishing is dominated by the United States. English has become the nearest thing to a world language. The worldwide spread of English-language culture, American and British, has resulted in English literature becoming known and studied more widely than any other.

As English spread around the world, local literatures in English developed, producing the modern situation where "English" literature is being written in North America, the Caribbean, Britain, Africa, Australia and New Zealand, Asia, and the Pacific region. Each literature has developed a distinctive voice. Canadian literature exists in both English and French, reflecting the history and linguistic make-up of the country. V.S. Naipaul, a Trinidadian of Indian descent, writes in English, as does the Nigerian Wole Soyinka. Ruth Prawer Jhabvala is Polish by birth, Indian by marriage, and a writer in English. On the other hand, the playwright Samuel Beckett, born in Ireland in 1906, writes in French more often than in English.

Writers have not been truly international since Latin ceased to be the common language of Europe's scholars more than two hundred years ago. But the communications revolution that created the so-called "global village" has helped to create an international market not just for TV soap operas but also for books.

⑧ Writers and Writing

Writers approach their task in different ways. Many successful authors follow a regular routine—writing for so many hours each day, perhaps. Some are perfectionists; James Joyce was reputed to ponder for a day over a single phrase. A modern bestseller-writer such as ex-jockey Dick Francis has to produce a new book nearly every year, to satisfy his publisher.

The Welsh poet Dylan Thomas said that every experience was both a thing and a word at the same time, both amazing. Writing, he said, could be like "carrying a huge armful of words to a table upstairs and wondering if he would reach it in time." Getting started can be a problem for the young writer. A good beginning is to keep a diary, noting down not only incidents and events, but also descriptions of mood, reaction, and character. Training the ear to catch dialogue, on a bus or in a store, is also valuable. Many writers have been dedicated letter-writers, their correspondence providing a treasure trove of information for later biographers.

There is no obvious path to becoming a professional writer. Studying literature at school or at college will not of itself turn someone into a literary genius. However, every writer learns from the experience and technique of others; writing is an imitative art. Most good books are based on solid research; it is difficult to write a novel set in a hospital if you have never been inside one. Even so, a writer does not need to experience everything (although some have tried). For example, novelists have written about murder without committing murder themselves, but few authors can write with honesty and conviction about something as powerful as love or the loss of a loved one without personal experience.

Salman Rushdie has become one of the most widely known modern novelists. He was born in Bombay, India, in 1947, went to school in England and afterward to Cambridge University. Torn between two cultures, he became a writer of magazine articles and a fringe actor. His first novel was a flop, selling only half its print run of 1,750 copies. His second novel, *Midnight's Children*, won the 1981 Booker Prize for fiction, sold 40,000 copies, and transformed Rushdie's life. *The Satanic Verses* (1988) outraged the Muslim world because of its allegedly blasphemous content, and was banned in Islamic countries. Rushdie's life was threatened and the author became the center of an international controversy over a writer's freedom and our attitudes toward the publication of books that cause offense to some people.

A book may arouse controversy if it breaches laws governing national security. Peter Wright's *Spycatcher* was banned by the British

Australia 'to seek ban' on MI5 agent's book

Send him to hell, says Khomeini

NO MERCY FOR RUSHDIE

RUSHDIE: Said he was sorry

government in 1987, for example. In dictatorships, writers have often come acrop of censorship laws. Democracies generally allow writers greater freedom. Is the pen mightier than the sword, as has been claimed? Some writers have doubted that books have any influence on events. Yet in the 1930s the Nazi Party feared ideas enough to burn books containing views they opposed. Chinese writers were persecuted during the Cultural Revolution of the 1960s, and until recently in the Soviet Union, the books of Solzhenitsyn were banned and writers who dared to criticize the Soviet government, such as Andrei Sinyavsky and Yuly Daniel, were jailed. Prior to the reform movement of 1990, some writers in Poland, such as Czeslaw Milosz, were forced to emigrate, others were banned. This continues to be the fate of writers in countries with repressive governments.

Most aspiring writers labor in obscurity, receiving only rejection slips and not checks from publishers. Others combine writing with other full-time jobs. The American poet Wallace Stevens, for instance, was an executive in an insurance company, Barbara Pym (novelist) and Stevie Smith (poet) lived, apparently uneventfully, as working women in London. Helen Hooven Santmyer (whose 1982 novel . . . *And Ladies of the Club* took fifty years to write) worked as a secretary in New York, then as a teacher and librarian. She was an elderly resident of a nursing home by the time she put the finishing touches to her book, which she wrote in longhand in a bookkeeper's ledger. Miles Franklin, author of *My Billiant Career* (1900), was brought up in the Australian bush, but rebelled against the narrowness of outback society. She lived for many

Above *Attempts to ban books inevitably attract more publicity (and readers). The writer's freedom of expression may be challenged by governments or by people whose religious or moral beliefs are offended.*

years in the United States and Britain, working as a social worker and for the feminist movement.

Few modern writers are also adventurers, roaming the world as did Jack London, Joseph Conrad, Ernest Hemingway, and others. For some, a trip to a writers' convention may be the farthest they travel from their word processors. Kenneth Grahame worked in a bank and wrote *The Wind in the Willows* in his spare time. The poet T.S. Eliot also worked for a bank for a time. Once they were away from their work their imaginations could function, differently, but with great effect.

For years, there have been gloomy predictions about the future of the book. No one reads any more, say the prophets of doom. But more books are published every year, and there is an ever-growing demand for literature of every kind. This is especially true of the developing countries of the world where newly literate people are hungry for knowledge. So great is this demand that there is a huge trade in "pirate" (illegally printed) copies of foreign books, ranging from sets of encyclopedias to the latest thriller fiction.

Today, literature is an art, a profession, a business, and an academic discipline. Writers come into fashion and are then relegated to the bottom shelf for a few more years. Teachers no longer expect their students to be able to read Homer and Virgil in their original Greek and Latin, but the plays of Shakespeare are pored over word for word by scholars and analyzed with the aid of computers.

A book, a poem, or a play can be enjoyed by anyone, at any level. The deeper you probe, the more surprises you may find; you may recognize a shared experience in the author's words and say to yourself: "That's just how it is." The literature that we read survives not because we are "taught" about it, but because for every new generation it continues to have relevance and meaning.

Below *New technologies have not challenged the book as humanity's most enduring source of information and enjoyment. Libraries, large and small, are a vital asset to a civilized society.*

Glossary

Allegory A story that has an apparently simple meaning but symbolizes a deeper truth.

Ballad A story in verse that describes a legendary or historical event.

Couplet Two lines of verse that directly follow each other and are rhymed.

Elegy A poem written in mourning after a death.

Enlightenment A philosophical movement of the eighteenth century that stressed the importance of reason and the reappraising of existing ideas.

Epic A long narrative poem that relates great heroic events, such as Virgil's *Aeneid*.

Essay A literary work in prose that allows the writer to comment on a particular subject.

Fable A moral tale with a message; animal characters often act out human situations.

Free verse Poetry written without formal meter.

Fringe theater Theater that is not part of the "establishment" or the commercial theater.

Genre Category or style, referring especially to an artistic work.

Hieroglyphics The characters used in ancient Egyptian picture writing.

Limerick Humorous rhyming verse—the nonsense verse of Edward Lear, for example.

Lyric Poetry that expresses a poet's innermost feelings and thoughts.

Masque A drama with music that was popular in seventeenth-century Europe.

Metaphor A word or expression that describes something as being what it resembles. For example, a ferocious man may be called a tiger.

Metaphysical Relating to seventeenth-century poets who combined intense feeling with ingenious thought and wrote with elaborate imagery.

Narrative The "story" element in any work of literature.

Neoclassical literature That literature modeled on the great works of the ancient Greeks and Romans.

Ode A poem written in praise of someone or something, and intended, in some cases, to be sung.

Oratory Speech-making.

Parody A work that makes fun of serious writing through imitation of it.

Poet laureate A poet honored for his achievements by a country or region.

Prologue An introduction—in a play this would be a long opening speech.

Romance Any narrative work dealing with events and characters remote from life.

Romanticism The theory, practice, and style of Romantic art, a movement in art, music, and literature of the late eighteenth and early nineteenth centuries.

Saga Epic literature of medieval northern Europe, particularly Iceland.

Satire Literature that ridicules the vices and follies of the world.

Simile An exact likening of one thing to another, for example, "the man fought like a tiger."

Soliloquy A theatrical device—the act of speaking to oneself.

Sonnet A poem of fourteen lines, following one of two rhyme-schemes—the Petrarchan (or Miltonic) and the Shakespearean.

Stream of consciousness An attempt to represent thought in writing by putting down ideas, feelings, and impressions as they might come to a character's mind.

Symbolism Writing that seeks to express a state of mind through the use of images.

Vernacular Describes the native language spoken by the people of a country.

Further Reading

There are many, many sources of great literature. The list below is intended to be a guide in your search and show you some of what is available.

Great American Short Stories by Editors WALLACE STEGNER and MARY STEGNER (Dell, 1985).

The Modern World: Ten Great Writers by MALCOLM BRADBURY (Penguin, 1989).

Native American Reader: Speeches, Poems & Stories of the American Indian by JERRY BLANCHE (Denali, 1989).

The Norton Anthology of Afro-American Literature, by HENRY L. GATES; et al, eds. (Norton, 1990)

The Norton Anthology of American Literature, Vols. I & II, 2nd ed. by NINA BAYM, et al, eds. (Norton, 1985).

The Norton Anthology of World Masterpieces, Vols. I & II, 5th ed. by Editor MAYNARD MACK (Norton, 1985).

Index

Page numbers in **bold** type refer to illustrations.

Picture acknowledgments

The author and publishers wish to thank the following for their help in supplying pictures; Bridgeman Art Library 22 (top); Mick Ross/Cephas Picture Library 22 (lower); David Cumming 8 (lower); Mary Evans 7, 14 (top), 15, 18 (top), 23 (lower), 25, 26 (top and lower left); 27, 31, 34, 38 (lower); John Frost Historical Pictures 44; Hulton Picture Library 13, 16, 18 (lower), 36 (top), 39 (lower); Kobal Collection 8 (top), 28, 29, 30 (lower), 39 (top); National Portrait Gallery 13 (lower), 26 (lower right); National Theatre 33; Ann and Bury Peerless 10 (top); RSC/Donald Cooper 35 (top); Ronald Sheridan 4, 9, 18 (lower); Topham 10 (lower), 14 (lower), 21, 35 (lower), 37, 42 (top); Wayland Picture Library 6, 11, 13 (top), 18, 24 (top and lower), 30 (top), 38 (top), 42 (lower), 45; Zefa 17 (top), 23 (top). Cover The Dickens House, London.
The illustration on page 27 (top) is reprinted by permission of Charles Scribner's Sons, an imprint of Macmillan Publishing Co. from *Treasure Island* by Robert Louis Stevenson, illustrated by N.C. Wyeth. Copyright 1911 Charles Scribner's Sons; copyright renewed 1939 N.C. Wyeth. Photograph supplied by Brandywine River Museum, Pa.